Weekly Reader Books presents

Heroes of the Civil War

Jefferson Davis

By Susan Dye Lee

Illustrated by Len W. Meents

 CHILDRENS PRESS, CHICAGO

This book is a presentation of Weekly Reader Books.
Weekly Reader Books offers book clubs for children from
preschool to young adulthood.

For further information write to:
Weekly Reader Books
1250 Fairwood Ave.
Columbus, Ohio 43216

Library of Congress Cataloging in Publication Data

Lee, Susan.
   Jefferson Davis.

   (Heroes of the Civil War)
   SUMMARY: A brief biography of the statesman who
served as President of the Confederate States of America
during the Civil War.
   1. Davis, Jefferson, 1808-1889—Juvenile literature.
2. Statesmen—United States—Biography—Juvenile
literature. 3. Confederate States of America—History
—Juvenile literature. [1. Davis, Jefferson, 1808-1889.
2. Statesmen] I. Meents, Len W. II. Title.
III. Series.
E467.1.D26L4   973.7'13'0924 [B]   77-20054
ISBN 0-516-04702-7

History is full of chance events. Take the case of Jefferson Davis and Abraham Lincoln. They were born only eight months apart. They both spent their early years in western Kentucky. And they both lived on farms within a hundred miles of one another.

Then, their lives went in very different directions. Davis moved south—Lincoln moved north. Davis got a college education—Lincoln had to educate himself. Davis became a rich cotton planter—Lincoln became a successful lawyer. Davis owned slaves—Lincoln did not.

Fifty-two years passed. Then, chance turned these two men into enemies. In 1861, a Civil War broke out between the North and South. At that time, Abraham Lincoln was President of the United States. And Jefferson Davis was President of the Confederate States. Each president wanted victory for his side. But only one could win.

Abraham Lincoln
United States of
America

Jefferson Davis
Confederate States of
America

Jefferson Davis was born June 3, 1808, on a farm in southern Kentucky. He was the tenth child of Samuel and Jane Davis. The parents named their youngest child after Thomas Jefferson, the third President of the United States.

Jefferson's father was a farmer. He grew wheat, corn, and tobacco. He also raised fine horses.

Samuel Davis did not work alone. He owned slaves to help him. At this time, slavery was still legal in the southern states of our nation. Kentucky was one of these slave states.

The Davis family moved to Mississippi before Jefferson was two. Samuel Davis hoped to make a lot of money there. He grew cotton, the main crop in the south.

Jefferson enjoyed his Mississippi home. His brother Isaac taught him to fish and ride. His sister Lucinda read him stories and poems.

Jefferson began school when he was five years old. Every day he walked a mile to a one-room, log-cabin school.

Jefferson's father wanted a better school for his son. So he sent him to St. Thomas, a boarding school in Kentucky. Jefferson studied reading and writing. He also learned Latin, math, and history. He was a good pupil.

Jefferson entered college when he was only 13. In 1821, he became a pupil at Transylvania University in Lexington, Kentucky. The classes at Transylvania were very hard. But Jefferson studied long hours and got good grades.

In 1824, Jefferson received a high honor. He was chosen to attend the United States Military Academy at West Point, New York.

West Point was a school for training army
officers. The students, called cadets, had to wear
uniforms. They could not smoke, drink, or play
cards.

Cadet Davis shared a small room with two other
cadets. He slept on a mattress on the floor. Water
for washing came from a pump outside. The
room had to be clean at all times.

The school day at West Point was very long. At sunrise a bugle woke the cadets for roll call. After breakfast, the cadets spent the morning in class. In the hour before lunch, they had to study.

The afternoon classes lasted only two hours. Then the cadets practiced shooting, riding, and marching. After supper, the cadets studied in their rooms. All lights had to be out by ten o'clock.

Cadet Davis became a hero in his weapons class. One day, the students were learning to make fire-balls. The fuse of one of the balls accidently became lit. Jefferson picked up the fire-ball and threw it out the window. His quick action saved many lives.

Jefferson Davis spent four years at West Point. He graduated on July 12, 1828, with the rank of second lieutenant. Now 20 years old, Lieutenant Davis stood nearly six feet tall. He looked every inch a soldier—trim, fit, and proud.

After a three-month vacation, Lieutenant Davis reported to Fort Crawford, an army outpost on the Wisconsin River. Fox, Sioux, and other Indian tribes lived nearby. French fur-trappers and hardy pioneers had also settled in the area.

Lieutenant Davis had many jobs. He directed repairs on the fort. He was put in charge of building a sawmill. He led scouting parties through the wilderness. On these trips, the soldiers lived off the land, eating corn, wild rice, fish, and game.

Sometimes Lieutenant Davis and his men were in danger from Indians. Tribes such as the Comanche did not like outsiders on their hunting grounds. Davis understood. He tried to stay on friendly terms with the Indians.

But peace came to an end in 1832. A tribe of Sacs were not happy at being pushed off their land. They wanted to return to their village. That spring, Chief Black Hawk and his people crossed the Mississippi River into Illinois.

The army ordered Black Hawk to return to Iowa. But he would not turn back. The army then began to hunt the Indians down.

In August, the army caught up with Black

Hawk's tribe at Bad Axe. The Indians raised a
white flag of truce. The soldiers attacked anyway.
They killed 150 men, women, and children. But
Black Hawk got away.

   Lieutenant Davis was ordered to find Black
Hawk. At last, two enemy Indian chiefs captured
Black Hawk. They then turned him over to Davis.
Black Hawk was put in prison at Fort Monroe in
Virginia.

Jefferson Davis was not proud of the army's war against Black Hawk. In his view, "The real heroes were Black Hawk and his savages."

Jefferson Davis began to question army life. At 27, he had spent seven years in the army, with little to show for it. Besides, he wanted to get married. But a frontier outpost was no place for a woman. Nor could Davis support a wife on army pay.

Jefferson talked the problem over with his brother Joseph. Joseph offered Jefferson 1,800 acres of his own land. With Joseph's help, Jefferson made up his mind to try farming in Mississippi.

In 1835, Jefferson Davis left the army. That
same year, on June 17, he and Sarah Knox Taylor
were married. They began life together in
Mississippi.

For two months, all went well. Then, Jefferson
and Sarah caught malaria. They both had fever
and chills. There was little the doctors could do.
On September 15, Sarah died in her husband's
arms.

The death of his young bride shattered the dreams of Jefferson Davis. He kept very much to himself. He spent long hours reading.

After months of sadness, Davis once again took an interest in farming. With the help of slaves, he planted cotton, his main crop. He also grew rice, corn, and other vegetables. Like his father, Davis liked to raise fine horses.

Davis named his plantation "Brierfield." In 1835, he built a one-story house. On either side of the house were cabins for the slaves. In back were stables, barns, chicken coops, and a smokehouse.

Davis ran his plantation with slave labor. He did not question this practice. He had grown up with slavery, and was used to it. He believed in it. In his view, slavery was as good for blacks as whites.

Davis lived alone for many years. Then, in 1845, he remarried. His second wife was Varina Howell. In time, they had six children.

One year later, the United States went to war with Mexico. The two countries were fighting over land. They did not agree on the boundary line of Texas.

Jefferson Davis joined a group of American soldiers called the "Mississippi Rifles." The soldiers chose Davis as their Colonel.

Colonel Davis fought with skill and courage in the Mexican War. He and his men helped capture the Mexican city of Monterey. At Buena Vista, American forces drove off an attack from Mexican troops. In that battle, Colonel Davis was badly wounded. At great risk, he stayed on the battlefield.

Colonel Davis returned home to a hero's welcome. Newspapers all over the country praised his bravery under enemy fire.

Davis's war record won him people's trust. He served in the United States Senate until 1851. From 1853 to 1857, he worked for President Franklin Pierce. It was Davis's job to keep the nation safe. He was in charge of the army and navy. His duties kept him very busy.

In 1857, Jefferson Davis was again elected to the Senate by the people of Mississippi. It was a difficult time to hold office. Differences over slavery were tearing the nation apart.

In the North, many people thought slavery was wrong. They did not want slavery to move westward. They wanted the new lands in the west to become free states.

Many southerners did not agree. They believed slavery was right. They wanted new lands in the west to become slave states.

Senator Davis spoke in the Senate for the southern point of view. But he also had many northern friends. He wanted the North and South to solve their problems peacefully. "Civil War has only horror for me," he told a friend.

Then, in 1860, Abraham Lincoln was elected president. Many in the South did not want a president who disliked slavery. Some slave-owners feared Lincoln would set their slaves free.

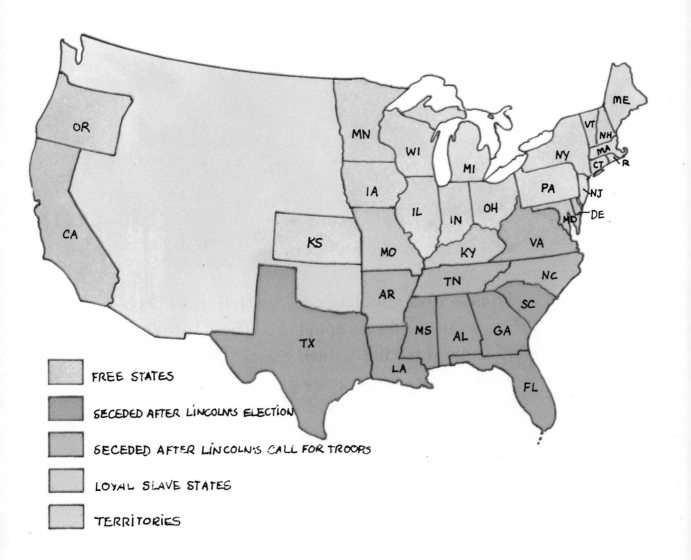

FREE STATES

SECEDED AFTER LINCOLN'S ELECTION

SECEDED AFTER LINCOLN'S CALL FOR TROOPS

LOYAL SLAVE STATES

TERRITORIES

After Lincoln's election, seven southern states dropped out of the Union. They did not want to be part of the United States any longer. In 1861, they formed a new government. It was called the Confederate States of America.

The Confederate States elected Jefferson Davis their president. He accepted the office. In spite of good feelings for the United States, Davis's loyalty to the South was stronger.

Would the United States let the southern states leave the Union? President Davis was not sure. He hoped for independence without a fight. He wanted the United States and Confederate States to live together in peace.

Instead, the North and South went to war. The fighting began April 12, 1861, at Fort Sumter, South Carolina. News of the battle spread quickly. Men on both sides signed up for army duty.

And so two men, each born in Kentucky 52 years earlier, now faced each other in war. Once again, they lived only 100 miles apart. President Lincoln headed the United States government in Washington, D.C. President Davis headed the Confederate government in Richmond, Virginia.

President Davis worked hard for independence. Four more states joined the Confederacy. Men had to be drafted into the army. Soldiers needed guns, clothing, and food. Money was short and the people had to be taxed. It was not easy to run a new government during wartime.

For a while, the war went well for the South.
They had good military leaders, like Robert E. Lee
and Stonewall Jackson. Southern armies won
battles at Malvern Hill and Bull Run. In 1862,
victory seemed close at hand.

Then, in June of 1863, General Lee's army lost
an important battle at Gettysburg, Pennsylvania.
At the same time, the riverport of Vicksburg,
Mississippi, fell to Union troops. These defeats
badly hurt southern chances for independence.

Slowly, the South began to wear down. The
Confederacy did not have enough factories. Goods
ran short. Without a good navy, the South could
not get supplies from England or Europe. Prices
rose sky-high.

By 1865, all hope for the South was gone. Now, the government of President Davis was in danger. Union troops wanted to capture Richmond. General Lee made his last stand outside the Confederate capital.

On April 1, Lee's army lost the battle for Richmond. Union forces began to close in. The city was not safe for the southern leaders.

The next day, President Davis and other government officials were forced to leave. Shortly after, Union troops marched into Richmond. President Lincoln arrived also. He walked through the ruins of the fallen capital. To the cheers of Union soldiers, he sat in Jefferson Davis's desk chair.

For the next month, President Davis moved his government farther and farther south. Along the way, he learned of General Lee's surrender to General Grant. The South had lost its fight for independence.

Palm Sunday
April 9, 1865 An
awed stillness come
to Appomattox
After four years of
unequal struggle
The South Surrender

President Davis knew the war was over. Yet he would not give up. "I cannot feel like a beaten man," he told one of his aides.

On April 19, President Davis learned of the murder of President Lincoln. But there was something he did not then know. Some government officials accused Davis of planning the crime. A reward of $100,000.00 had been offered for the capture of the Confederate president!

President Davis had nothing to do with the murder of President Lincoln. But Union soldiers did not know this. They wanted the reward money. They began hunting for the fleeing Confederate leader.

Union soldiers accidently discovered President Davis near Irwinsville, Georgia, on May 10. They captured him, his wife, and his family. It was then Davis learned of the reason for a price on his head.

The ex-president of the Confederate States was put in prison. He was locked in Fort Monroe with his legs in iron chains. He was kept there two years without a trial. He became very sick.

Jefferson Davis was never put on trial. In time, many northerners began to feel sorry for Davis. In May of 1867, he was let out of prison on bail.

The rest of Jefferson Davis's life was very hard. He had lost everything during the war. His health was poor. He had very little money and no way to make a living.

The Civil War ended Jefferson Davis's old way of life. Slavery and plantation life were over. The Davis family was uprooted. They tried living in many places—Canada, England, and Tennessee.

At last, the family settled in Louisiana. There,
Jefferson Davis wrote *The Rise and Fall of the
Confederate Government.* It was a history of Davis's
government during the Civil War years.

Jefferson Davis died at age 81, on December 6, 1889. The news of his death saddened many southerners. They recalled his kindness, loyalty, and devotion to duty. They remembered his dignity in the face of defeat. They praised his courage during the years in prison. They were proud of him.

Jefferson Davis was a symbol of the South. He had been its leader in the fight for independence. He stood for a way of life gone forever. The South would always remember him as the first and only President of the Confederate States of America.

IMPORTANT DATES

1808	Jefferson Davis is born in Christian (now Todd) County, Kentucky.
1809	Abraham Lincoln is born in Hardin (now Larue) County, Kentucky.
1810?	Davis family moves to Wilkinson County, Mississippi.
1821	Jefferson Davis goes to Transylvania University in Lexington, Kentucky.
1824-1828	Jefferson Davis goes to West Point.
1828	Second Lieutenant Davis serves in the army.
1832	Davis fights in the Black Hawk War.
1835	Jefferson Davis leaves the army and marries Sarah Knox Taylor. She dies two months later.
1835-1845	Jefferson Davis stays on his plantation, Brierfield.
1845	Jefferson Davis marries Varina Howell and is elected to the U.S. House of Representatives.
1846	Davis fights in the Mexican War.
1847-1851	Davis elected U.S. Senator from Mississippi.
1853-1857	Davis is appointed Secretary of the War; Franklin Pierce is President of the United States.
1857-1861	Davis elected U.S. Senator; he fights for the rights of the South.
1861	Abraham Lincoln is President of the United States; Davis leaves the Senate; Mississippi secedes from the Union.
1861	Jefferson Davis named President of the Confederate States on February 18; fighting begins at Fort Sumter, Charleston, South Carolina, on April 12.
1862	Southern army victorious in the Shenandoah Valley and at Bull Run.
1863	July 1-3, the Battle of Gettysburg; General Lee's army defeated.
1865	April 3, Jefferson Davis flees Richmond; April 9, General Robert E. Lee surrenders to General Grant at Appomattox Court House in Virginia; April 15, Abraham Lincoln dies.
1865	May 10, Jefferson Davis taken prisoner at Irwinville, Georgia.
1865-1867	Davis is in prison at Fort Monroe.
1867	Jefferson Davis released on bond from Fort Monroe.
1878-1881	Wrote *The Rise and Fall of the Confederate Government*.
1889	December 6, Jefferson Davis dies and is buried in New Orleans. In 1893 his body is moved to Richmond, Virginia.

About the Author

Susan Dye Lee enjoys a varied career as historian, teacher, and writer. After studying history and English at DePauw University, she began teaching and writing professionally in 1961. Working with the Social Studies Curriculum Center at Northwestern University, she created course materials in conjunction with her teaching responsibilities. Ms. Lee has also co-authored a text on Latin America and Canada, helped develop case studies in legal history for the Law in American Society Project, and written numerous filmstrips and teacher's guides for audio-visual materials in American history. For Childrens Press, she and her husband, John R. Lee, co-authored a series of books on the American Revolution, which they completed shortly before Dr. Lee's death in 1976.

Ms. Lee's special interest is women in history. She has developed a filmstrip series on the sex roles of men and women, as well as teaching courses on the topic. Currently, she is completing her history dissertation on the Woman's Christian Temperance Union for Northwestern University.

In her free moments, Susan Lee enjoys traveling, playing the piano, and reading. During the summer, she explores northern Wisconsin from her cottage in Woodruff. A native of Cincinnati, Ohio, Ms. Lee presently makes her home in Evanston, Illinois.

About the Artist

Len Meents studied painting and drawing at Southern Illinois University and after graduation in 1969 he moved to Chicago. Mr. Meents works full time as a painter and illustrator. He and his wife and child currently make their home in LaGrange, Illinois.